DWIGHT GOODEN

★

DALE MURPHY

Jordan Deutsch

AVON SUPERSTARS

AVON BOOKS
A division of
The Hearst Corporation
1790 Broadway
New York, New York 10019

Copyright © 1986 by Avon Books
Published by arrangement with the author
ISBN: 0-380-75115-1

All rights reserved, which includes the right to
reproduce this book or portions thereof in any form
whatsoever except as provided by the U. S. Copyright Law.
For information address Avon Books.

First Avon Printing, May 1986

AVON TRADEMARK REG. U. S. PAT. OFF. AND IN OTHER
COUNTRIES, MARCA REGISTRADA, HECHO EN
U. S. A.

Printed in the U. S. A.

OPM 10 9 8 7 6 5 4 3 2 1

Avon Books are available at special quantity discounts for
bulk purchases for sales promotions, premiums, fund raising
or educational use. Special books, or book excerpts, can
also be created to fit specific needs.

For details write or telephone the office of the Director of
Special Markets, Avon Books, Dept. FP, 1790 Broadway,
New York, New York 10019, 212-399-1357.

The author wishes to acknowledge the following:

Dwight Gooden and Richard Woodley from their work, *Rookie*, published by Doubleday

Sports Illustrated magazine

The Baseball Hall of Fame

Inside Sports magazine

DWIGHT GOODEN

1

From the Little League to the Rookie League

Dwight was born on November 16, 1964, in Tampa, Florida, and is the youngest of his parents' 3 children. Although he is the only boy of Dan and Ella's marriage, he has 3 older brothers by his father's former marriage.

Dwight met his first major leaguer when he was 6 years old. When Dwight was 6, his dad, Dan Gooden, drove over from their home in Tampa to the Detroit Tigers' spring training camp in Lakeland, Florida. And Dwight found himself sitting on the lap of Al Kaline, the future Hall of Famer! Afterward, Kaline hit 2 home runs in the exhibition game. Dwight was so impressed that he wanted to play the outfield and hit home runs just like Al Kaline, the right fielder who became his idol.

Dwight did not really start playing baseball until he was 10. But even then, his natural abilities were good enough to have him play with kids who were 11 and 12. He played third base, and his team won the Florida championship and went to the annual Little League World Series in Williamsport, Pennsylvania. But Dwight was not eligible to play. You had to be at least 11!

Back then, Dwight not only played baseball, but basketball and football as well. Although he still enjoys playing basketball in the off-season, any thoughts of playing football quickly went out the window when someone stepped on his hand and broke his wrist.

By the time he got to be 11, he was still playing third base. But now his arm was getting well developed from all the throws he made from third. By the time he reached age 12, he was also pitching, striking out batters at a furious pace. In one game alone, he not only struck out 16 of 18 batters in a seven-inning game, but also hit 2 home runs! In that same incredible outing, he didn't give up any hits or walks, and Dwight was credited with an "official" Little League perfect game!

While Dwight was fortunate to have his father (a former semipro baseball player who also managed a semipro team) around to give him advice, he also gives a lot of credit to his high school coach Billy Reed, who, as Dwight now says, "was probably the toughest coach I ever had. He really knew how to develop young ballplayers. And he never let you rest on your laurels. He always forced you to use all your talents."

But while Coach Reed helped Dwight find different ways to throw his fastball and get better rotation on his curve, Dwight is quick to recognize the great role both of his parents played in helping him gain the poise and maturity needed to survive in the tough game of major league baseball. "My dad helped make me a ballplayer by teaching me to take the good with the bad, and my mom helped with developing a good attitude and keeping an even temper. She reminded me that people are always watching, and how stupid it looks to be carrying on."

By the time Dwight got to his junior year at Hillsborough High, his reputation was really growing. But even so, he was unable to become a starter right away, because, as Dwight says, "It was a team loaded with talent." And he is right. Included on the roster were Al Everett (drafted by the Twins), Vance Lovelance

8

(first-round pick of the Cubs) and Floyd Youmans (a promising young pitcher who was originally signed by the Mets, but who was traded to the Expos in the Gary Carter–Hubie Brooks trade). But by the time the annual high school Easter Tournament was over, Dwight, who was mostly a reliever and third baseman, was named MVP of the tournament. His record for the season was 7–0 with an incredible 0.76 ERA!

That summer, Dwight got his now-famous nickname while pitching in a summer league. After one of his teammates yelled, "Operate on him, Doc," the nickname stuck. As "Doc" got ready for his senior year, he had already started thinking of making baseball a career. The Pittsburgh Pirates' scouts had been to see him a couple of times and liked the way he swung the bat. They were thinking of him for third base or the outfield. Not for pitching!

In his senior year, with the scouts of the Cincinnati Reds, Chicago Cubs and California Angels joining the chase, Dwight hit a solid .340 but had only a 7–4 pitching record. Because he knew that he'd have a better chance of making it to the majors as a pitcher, he figured he wouldn't go too high in the draft. But Dwight did not consider that, along with his 7–4 record, he had struck out an awesome 135 batters in only 74 innings and had a microscopic 0.35 ERA—less than ½ a run for every 9 innings pitched.

While waiting for the June 7 draft, Dwight got a scholarship offer from the University of Miami. It was something that really delighted his mom, since she couldn't really understand baseball's being a profession. Dwight decided that if he didn't get drafted in the first 5 rounds, then he would skip becoming a pro at that time and go to college instead. When the big day approached, one of the reporters from the Tampa *Tribune* who knew Dwight asked if he wanted to come

9

to the newspaper office and watch the draft come across on the computer. Of course, Dwight gave a big YES, and the next day went down with a friend to see what his future would be.

Dwight and his friend were treated to juice and doughnuts, compliments of the *Tribune*, and then the computer started up. The first pick in the nation was Shawson Dunston, a slugging high school third baseman from Brooklyn who is now the starting shortstop for the Chicago Cubs. But then, as Dwight was trying to pay attention to the next few names, his mind went blank in all the excitement. There it was on the screen, the number five pick in the nation, Dwight Gooden ...New York Mets! He just couldn't believe it. "I thought I was dreaming." (It seems incredible now, but 3 other teams skipped Dwight in the draft. The Toronto Blue Jays, the San Diego Padres and the Minnesota twins chose, in order, infielder Augie Schmidt, pitcher Jimmy Jones and pitcher Bryan Oelkers.)

Dwight even had the reporter call New York to make sure that there wasn't "some other Dwight Gooden someplace." But it was no mistake, and by the time Dwight got home, the word was everywhere. The phone didn't stop ringing as newspaper reporters and radio and television people were trying to arrange interviews. Even his friend Floyd Youmans, who finished high school in California, called. But Floyd was calling to say he'd been picked by the Mets in the second round. "When I told him what round I had been picked, he thought I was teasing."

The next calls to the Gooden household came from agents. Dan Gooden picked 4 who sounded interesting and invited them over to the house. Finally Jim Neader, a lawyer from St. Petersburg, was chosen to represent Tampa's newest celebrity.

As a signing bonus, Neader was able to get Dwight

$85,000—plus expenses if he ever decided to go to college. For Dwight, the thought of having so much money at once made him dizzy. After all, his family wasn't rich. They lived in a middle-class black working neighborhood in East Tampa. But Dwight, still spinning from all the sudden fame, did not forget those nearest to him. He happily shared some of his bonus money with his family. And while his agent found some investments for Dwight, he did what any high school graduate would do with a large chunk of money. He went out and bought a shiny new car: a silver Camaro Z28!

It had been an incredible journey on what seemed like a rocket trip. Here he was, still 17, and signed to report to the major leagues. Even Dwight couldn't believe that he was about to enter professional baseball!

2

The Best Arm in the Minors

With a first-class airline ticket in his hand, and his
parents, sisters and friends waving good-bye, Dwight
was on his way to Kingsport in the Appalachian
League. After easily shutting out the opposition for
7 innings in his first start, he still felt as if he were
dreaming. And why not: in one week he had gone from
being drafted to his first professional start.

But in his next start, the dream quickly ended. He
gave up 7 runs in 2 innings. Dwight just couldn't
understand it. "My fastball was popping and my curve
was breaking well. I figured if my pitches were good,
I couldn't lose. But they hit everything I threw."

After the game he called his dad in Tampa, and was
reminded that there are some days that, no matter
how well you do, you lose. Even though Dwight tended
to be a perfectionist, he was learning that you just
can't win every game.

But Dwight settled down, and when the season had
ended he had been named to the rookie All-Star team,
and was selected as the best pitcher in the Appalachian League. It was such a strong performance that
the Mets decided to move him up to the New York–
Penn League in Little Falls, where the team was fighting for a pennant.

He made 2 starts and had a 0–1 record when all
the innings he had pitched between high school and
his new pro career finally took their toll. After telling
the Mets' minor league director that his arm was tired,
Dwight was sent to New York to see Dr. Parkes, the

Mets' team doctor. As things turned out, his arm was only suffering from overwork. But his trip to New York gave him the opportunity to see a major league stadium for the very first time. He just couldn't believe how beautiful Shea Stadium was, and it gave him an incentive to work even harder to get to the big leagues.

Dwight took his tired arm back to Tampa for a rest, and in the fall met and auditioned for George Bamberger, then the Mets' manager, and John Cumberland, who was the pitching coach at Lynchburg in the Class A Carolina League. They must have liked what they saw in Dwight, because by the time March rolled around, Dwight was promoted to Class A ball.

So here was Dwight, only 18, playing with guys who were 5 and 6 years older. But his fastball was now in the ninety-plus per hour range, and his confidence and experience grew with every game. After Dwight opened with a 3–2 record after 8 starts, his Lynchburg team came into Shea Stadium to play the Salem Redbirds, the Texas Rangers' Class A team.

It was only an exhibition game before the regular Mets' game, but those who were fortunate enough to be on hand got a glimpse of what was to come. Dwight was really pumped up, and threw a one-hitter while striking out 14 batters through 8 innings before running into trouble in the ninth when the Redbirds got an infield hit, a bunt and then another single to tie the game at 1–1. Dwight managed to get the next batter on strikes, but then gave up a home run and left the game losing 4–1. But those first 8 innings were a sign of things to come, and the loss did nothing to dampen his determination. He recovered to reel off 15 straight wins, and came within 1 out of throwing a no-hitter against Peninsula, the Phillies' farm team.

With a 19–4 mark and a league-record 300 strikeouts, Dwight was promoted to Tidewater, the Mets' top minor league team, toward the end of the season. It was a big jump from A to Triple A, and he was given a big assignment: he was called to help the Tides win the International League title.

In his first outing, he lost to Columbus, the Yankees' farm team, but he came back to beat Richmond, the Braves' team, which clinched the title for the Tides. Then, in the round-robin with Denver of the American Association, which is the White Sox's team, and Portland (the Phillies' team) in the Pacific Coast League, Dwight beat Portland 4–2 in the Triple A world series to help make Tidewater the overall champs of the minor leagues. As a final topping to the season, *Baseball America*, a minor league newspaper, named him Best Player in the Minors.

In looking back to the 1983 season, Dwight had proved to himself that he could pitch against the best the minors could offer. But, as spring training approached for the 1984 season, no one from the Mets' front office had talked to him about playing on the parent club. He thought he would have to pitch well at Tidewater for an entire season, or perhaps that the Mets would call him up sometime later, maybe around the All-Star break.

But what lay ahead for Dwight and the batters in the National League would not only surprise the 19-year-old fastballer from Tampa, but the rest of the baseball world as well.

3

On the Way to Shea

When Dwight arrived in the Mets' spring training camp in February, 1984, he had no idea that he would be part of the team's fortunes when the season opened that April. He was only invited to camp as a non-roster player; and to his thinking it was probably to gain more experience. But aside from the fine record he had posted in the minors, there were 2 things in his favor.

The Mets had failed to protect their old ace, Tom Seaver, who was plucked from their roster by the Chicago White Sox, and the team had a new manager in Davey Johnson. Johnson had seen Dwight when he was a roving scout in 1982—and of course at Tidewater, where Davey managed in 1983 when Dwight came up to the Triple A club and helped it win the minor league world series.

When Dwight made his first start in a scrimmage game, all eyes were on him, including those of Frank Cashen, the Mets' general manager. Dwight walked Wally Backman—also just up from Tidewater—but then struck out Ron Gardenhire and Danny Heep on curveballs and Hubie Brooks on a fastball! As Dwight says, "I felt great, mainly because nobody had scored off me." In the next inning he gave up a run on a walk and a hit, but then shut out the side in the third. His work was done for the day, and the other Mets—having ignored him before the game—now started to tease him in the way of professional athletes. Dwight didn't mind. He knew it was the players' way of telling him what a fine job he had done.

Dwight's next three-inning start came against the St. Louis Cardinals' B team, a mixture of reserves and regulars. Again, he did well. He then found himself facing the Toronto Blue Jays' regular team. The Mets were playing at Dunedin—which was close to Tampa—in the same stadium where Dwight had pitched in high school tournaments. To add to the pressure, his parents and a group of friends from high school were there.

"I was nervous facing big league hitters I had only watched on TV. I told myself, Just throw strikes." And he did. He got Willie Upshaw, the first batter, to ground out, but then he gave up a double to Ernie Witt on a 2–2 count and a home run to Cliff Johnson, the Jays' big power hitter. The home run shook Dwight, but he quickly settled down and retired the next 8 batters.

Davey Johnson then took him out when a nail on his index finger began to bleed. Dwight, as always, wanted to be perfect, but except for that home-run pitch, he had done a pretty good job. Davey and his coaches thought it had been a great outing for a 19-year-old kid.

In his next start, he pitched 4 innings against Toronto; and this time he held them to 2 hits and no walks with 3 strikeouts. Then came the Yankees. For Dwight, it was his biggest game. Not only was the crowd around 30,000—the largest of the spring training season—but the game was being televised back to New York. Dwight's pitching opponent was Ron Guidry. "He was the biggest name pitcher I had worked against. Just the two of us starting out against each other was a thrill."

Dwight went 5 innings and gave up 3 hits and only 1 run. One of the hits was a home run by Graig Nettles.

He had golfed a down-and-in change-up right out of the park. At the time, Dwight didn't know of Nettles' fondness for pitches that were off-speed and down. The Mets wound up winning in the ninth, 4–1; Dwight, knowing that he had only given up 1 run to the Yankees, thought that maybe he had made the team.

Of course, he kept such hopes to himself. But his performances did not escape the eyes of the press. Comparisons were being made to great pitching stars such as Nolan Ryan and Hall of Famer Bob Gibson. To some of the writers, it wasn't that he "might" but that he "should" make the team.

As the time for the regular season drew near, Dwight was one of 10 pitchers left in camp. But Johnson only planned on taking 9 to the big leagues. With no one telling Dwight what the decision would be, he had to wait and see if it would be him or pitcher Tim Leary going back to Tidewater.

On the last day of spring training, Dwight faced the Tigers for 1 scheduled inning. Two went down on strikes and the third flied out. When Dwight returned to the dugout, Johnson gave him the verdict. He was taking all 10 up North. For the start of the 1984 season, Dwight would be in the uniform of the New York Mets!

4
Rookie of the Year

The Mets opened the season with a loss to Cincinnati and then won 6 in a row. It was their best start since 1962, 2 years before Dwight was born! After finishing last in their division for the past 2 seasons, it looked like the Mets might be moving up. They were now headed for Houston, where they would play the Astros. Dwight would be pitching in the major leagues for the first time!

Naturally, Dwight was nervous. Instead of taking the team bus to the park, he decided to walk the mile and a half. By the time the game got started, he still found it hard to settle down. But when he retired the side in the first and recorded his first big league strikeout, fanning Dickie Thon, he began to feel confident. The one thing he wouldn't do, though, was look at his parents, who were sitting above the Mets' dugout. He knew that would make him too nervous.

Dwight left the game after the fifth inning, leading 3–1. It was all that Davey Johnson had wanted him to pitch in his first start. Davey didn't want to take a chance on hurting that valuable arm. Dwight had given up 3 hits and struck out 5. It was a grade-A first outing. Houston went on to score a run, but the Mets won 3–2 and Dwight had his first major league victory!

But in Dwight's next start against the Cubs at Wrigley Field, he ran into a lot of trouble. Chicago bombed him for 6 runs in less than 4 innings. He lost the game and wondered if he really belonged in the majors. When he spoke to his dad that night (something he does after every game he pitches), he realized that it was something he had to put behind him, to learn from his mistakes and get ready for the next time.

He did. But in his home opener at Shea Stadium against the Expos, he was the victim of an error and 4 unearned runs. The Mets won, but Dwight was not involved in the decision. A week later at Montreal, he held the Expos to 1 run in 7 innings, but again was not around when the Mets won in the eleventh. Still, he had recorded his first double-figure strikeout game by fanning 10 Expos!

It wasn't long before Mets fans started hanging a red "K" over the railing every time he struck out an opposing batter. Soon, a special spot in the upper left-field stands became known as the "K Korner" and the newspapers named Dwight "Dr. K."

The excitement of this teenage rookie from Tampa was beginning to spread around the league. Even the older players were amazed at his easygoing manner and ability. He was not only being compared to the best pitchers in both leagues, he was also being mentioned in the same breath as great pitchers from the past, such as Hall of Famer Bob Feller, a former teenage pitching sensation.

The only thing really bothering Dwight was the trouble he was having holding runners on base. It might be hard to hit against him, but it wasn't hard to steal against him. The trouble was, when Dwight had been pitching in Little League, high school and the minors, he never had to worry about men on base. Most of the time, there were none to worry about!

And Davey Johnson wasn't worried. Dwight was pitching so well that Davey didn't want to disturb his concentration, so he decided that they would wait until next year in spring training to work on Dwight's pickoff move.

Dwight was doing so well that by the time the All-Star break came around, he had a league-leading 133 K's and an 8–5 record. To many, it was no surprise when Dwight was picked for the All-Star team. But it was to Dwight, who said, "I can't believe I'm one of them. I wasn't even on the team in spring training, and 2 years ago I was in high school!" He was even more amazed when he found out that he was the youngest player ever selected for such an honor!

As Dwight got ready for the All-Star Game in Candlestick Park—the Giants' home in San Francisco—he couldn't have been happier. It was the All-Star break and the Mets were in first place. Dwight knew that the team leading at the break often won the division. He really hoped it would happen this year.

When the All-Star Game got under way, Paul Owens—the Phillies' manager who was managing the National League team—decided to start with Charlie Lea of the Expos and then Fernando Valenzuela of the Dodgers. Dwight would be the third pitcher.

Dwight began to warm up in the fourth, but he stopped and watched on every pitch Valenzuela threw. The Dodger screwballer struck out Dave Winfield, then Reggie Jackson and then George Brett! Dwight couldn't believe he had to follow such a performance. Here it was, the National League was leading 2–1, and Dwight had to start the fifth inning in relief of Valenzuela who had just struck out the side. To add a bit more tension, Dwight realized that he hadn't pitched in relief since high school!

After talking over his pitching selection with catcher Gary Carter (then with the Expos) he began to warm up. The first batter he faced was the dangerous Lance Parrish, the Tigers' home-run-hitting catcher. Dwight tried to settle down (not an easy task with over 50,000 screaming fans looking on), and he did when he struck out Parrish with a high fastball on a 2–2 count. He relaxed a little more when he got Chet Lemon, also of the Tigers, to swing at and miss a high fastball on a 1–2 count. The next batter up was the hard-hitting Alvin Davis of Seattle, who would go on to become the Rookie of the Year in the American League. Dwight gave Davis the same diet of fastballs and curves that he had given Parrish and Lemon, and had his third strikeout. He had fanned the side, just as Valenzuela had done!

When Dwight strode off the mound, he was walking on air. The appreciative crowd were on their feet. Dwight had helped establish a new All-Star Game record, and he didn't even know it. Between Dwight and the Dodger ace, they had struck out 6 in a row, 1 more than the old record established 50 years ago to the day by the New York Giants' Hall of Famer Carl Hubbell (who was in the ballpark as part of the Golden Anniversary celebration of his great pitching feat).

Dwight's All-Star performance brought the press out in greater number. Instead of just talking to him when he pitched, the 30 or so reporters assigned to cover baseball's teenage sensation also wanted interviews when he wasn't pitching!

The thing that really impressed the media was how Dwight could stay calm in tough situations—especially when he was only 19 and in his first year in the majors. Older players and observers of the game are amazed by Dwight's maturity and his ability to maintain his poise.

Dwight, though, doesn't see anything very special about the way he handles himself in a game: "When

I'm on the mound, I just do my best not to let anything bother me. I don't get emotional. Whether things are bad or great for me, I just try to keep the same attitude, the same expression on my face. I learned those lessons when I was small."

After the All-Star break, Dwight ran into some trouble against Atlanta, where he lost while striking out 10 Braves. Then, in Cincinnati, he had to leave the game after 9 innings with the score 2–2. He had recorded 11 strikeouts against the Reds. In his next 3 games, Dwight recorded 1 victory but lost games to St. Louis and Chicago.

Then, reaching back for something extra, he reeled off 7 victories in a row! In the sixth game of the streak, he came within a squib infield single of throwing a no-hitter against the Cubs! He missed the no-hitter, but he did strike out 11 Cubs, which raised his total to 235 and established a new National League mark for a rookie. The original record was established by Hall of Famer Grover Cleveland Alexander back in 1911.

In his very next game, he struck out 16 Pirates to establish a new major league record for strikeouts by a rookie—beating Herb Score's 1955 mark of 245 by 6 K's. And Dwight still had a few games left to pitch. In his next start, which came against the Phillies at Veterans Stadium, Dwight again struck out 16 batters. It gave him 2 more records. He tied Nolan Ryan's major league two-game consecutive strikeout record (32) and established a new National League record for 3 consecutive games with his 43 K's. The existing National League mark had been the sole possession of Hall of Famer Sandy Koufax since 1959. That was the good news. The bad news was that Dwight lost the game in a very frustrating manner in the eighth inning. First, he allowed a single to Shane Rawley, the Phillies' pitcher. Then he wild-pitched him to second base before an infield out moved him to third base. (If Dwight hadn't thrown the wild pitch, the infield out might have easily become a double play.) The home-plate umpire then charged Dwight with a "balk" and the run scored to give the Phillies a 2–1 win and snap Dwight's seven-game streak.

Dwight stopped the Expos on 5 hits in his last start of the season to run his record to 17–9. But as far as post-season play was concerned, Dwight and the rest of the Mets would have to watch the games from the sidelines. The Cubs easily won the division title by 6½ games after beating the Mets 4 straight in August. But with the Mets winning 90 games—their best mark since 1973—the team really had nothing to be sorry about. After all, they had discovered that the best pitching arm in baseball belonged to them. And he was still only a teenager.

As Dwight returned to Tampa to take a well-deserved rest, he could look back upon a year filled with important accomplishments. He had set a whole batch of records, finished tied for second in the National League for victories (17) with Cincinnati's Mario Soto (Joaquin Andujar of St. Louis posted 20), and he came in second in ERA with 2.60 to the Dodgers' Alexandro Peña, who had 2.48. He also led the league in strikeouts (276), which was the first time a teenage rookie had ever led the majors. Those strikeouts, by the way, gave him an average of 11.39 per 9 innings, which just happened to be a major league mark! The former record was set in 1965 when Cleveland's "Sudden" Sam McDowell averaged 10.71 strikeouts every 9 innings.

Dwight's efforts were rewarded with the Rookie of the Year award, of course, and he became the second Met in 2 years to win the honor. In 1983, Darryl Strawberry had won it. While the rookie award came as no

23

surprise, Dwight's being named runner-up to Rick Sutcliffe of Chicago for the Cy Young Award was a bit of a surprise! Sutcliffe, who came over to the Cubs from the Indians after the season started, posted a 16–1 mark in the National League. Dwight was also happy to be named, with Sutcliffe, to the UPI All-Star team.

Dwight was now recognized as an emerging superstar in the major leagues. And to think that only 7 months before, he was fighting for a spot on the Mets' pitching staff! To say that he had come a long way would be the understatement of the year. His growing fame also got him a commercial with former All-Star pitcher Catfish Hunter, for Diet Pepsi. Dwight had agreed to do shoe promotions for Nike Shoes (after trying on all the shoes of the competition), and a tie-in with Rawlings, the sporting goods manufacturer. He also did a poster for *Sports Illustrated*. But getting his picture on a baseball card probably gave Dwight the biggest thrill.

Dwight also did a few other things in the off-season. He attended banquets, the Mobil Baseball Clinic and the Mets' winter instructional league! Even with the unbelievable progress he had made, he knew that, to improve, he would have to develop a better pickoff move to hold runners on base and to alter his delivery to prevent having "balks" called on him.

When you realize that Dwight allowed the hitters in the National League a .202 batting average, compared to a combined .256 average for all other pitchers in 1984, it's easy to see why he's considered to be the prime candidate for a thirty-victory season. But to that, Dwight can only remark, "Thirty games ... I don't know. But it's nice of them to think I can."

5

The Best Is Yet to Come

As the 1985 season got under way, the Mets were feeling optimistic. Gary Carter, the leagues' top offensive catcher, had come over from Montreal in a trade for shortstop Hubie Brooks and some promising young ballplayers. After they had finished runner-up to the Cubs in 1984, Carter seemed to be the missing ingredient the Mets needed to go over the top. He could supply them with offensive punch with the bat and provide a steady hand behind the plate for the Mets' young pitching staff. And that young pitching staff led by Dr. K and Ron Darling, with a year of major league baseball under their belts, had the fans of New York hoping to celebrate their first National League pennant since 1973.

When the season opened on April 9, Dwight was on the mound against Joaquin Andujar of the Cardinals. And although Dwight wasn't around to figure in the decision (he had struck out 6 in 6⅔ innings and given up 2 earned runs), Carter saved the day for the Mets by hitting a dramatic home run in the bottom of the tenth to give the Mets the game, 6–5!

A few days later, in Dwight's next start, he struck out 10 Cincinnati batters and posted a complete-game shutout victory. If there were any thoughts that Dwight might face the sophomore jinx that hits so many second-year players, he quickly quieted those thoughts in his next game when he held the Phillies scoreless for over 8 innings on 3 hits! Jesse Orosco, the Mets' top reliever, came in to preserve the 1–0 victory.

Dwight took his 2–0 record to St. Louis where he again faced Andujar. This time, though, there were no late-inning heroics, and Dwight found himself saddled with his first loss. He had only given up 4 hits in 7 innings, but he still found himself at the bottom of a 5–1 score.

Dwight recovered in his next start, and overpowered the Astros 4–1, on 4 hits, and then beat the Reds at Cincinnati to help move the Mets into first place. On May 10, back at Shea, Dwight fired a three-hitter and beat Steve Carlton and the Phils, 5–0 on 13 K's, to run his record to 5–1. With Dwight pitching as brilliantly as he was, and with Gary Carter, Ron Darling and rookie reliever Roger McDowell adding key contributions, the Mets seemed ready to take permanent possession of first place. But on the next day, All-Star outfielder Darryl Strawberry tore up his thumb making a shoestring catch. Suddenly, the Mets found themselves without the services of one of their top home-run hitters. When the news came that Strawberry would be out for almost 2 months, the fans, who were coming to the stadium in record numbers, could only hope that the team would hang on until his return.

Dwight helped keep the Mets in the race with a victory over Houston on May 15, but then ran into 2 rough back-to-back losses (against San Diego and Los Angeles). Still, the Mets were tied with the Cubs for first. Then, at San Francisco, Dwight closed out the month of May with a 2–1, fourteen-strikeout performance. Not only had he taken over the league lead in strikeouts with 89, but he was also responsible for the Mets' moving into sole possession of first place. Yet, even with Dwight winning the next 2 games before running into a no-decision game at Montreal, the Mets were unable to hold onto the division lead. They had, in fact, dropped to fourth place behind the Cubs, St. Louis and the Expos. Although Dwight was able to pick up his third shutout of the season against the Cubs and then run his record to 11–3 when he beat Chicago later in the week, the team could do no better than finish the month of June in third place. In the topsy-turvy race, the surprising Cardinals were now in first with Montreal second. St. Louis wasn't supposed to challenge the Mets and Cubs after losing the great relief pitcher Bruce Sutter to the Atlanta Braves. The "experts" who make predictions must have forgotten about Willie McGee and Jack Clark. And who was that Vince Coleman kid, anyway?

Dwight had closed out the month with another no-decision at St. Louis. He had held the Cardinals to 5 hits in 8 innings in what turned out to be a 2–1 eleventh-inning loss for the Mets. Then, in his next start, he posted still another no-decision against the Braves in Atlanta. This time, though, it turned out to be one of the strangest baseball games ever played.

Dwight was taken out in the third inning due to 2 rain delays because Davey Johnson was afraid that his arm would tighten from too much sitting. Dwight then watched the Mets and the Braves play a nineteen-inning game that took 6 hours and 10 minutes to complete. The Mets scored 5 runs in the top of the nineteenth inning to finally win the game 16–13. The time was 5 minutes to 4 in the morning! Since the game had started on July 4, and fireworks had been promised after the game, the few hundred loyal Braves fans still on hand were given their treat of multicolored rockets and flares, even if it was July 5!

Although Dwight was able to win the rest of the games he pitched in July, and recorded his sixteenth victory (with only 3 losses), the Mets—with Strawberry now back in action—could do no better than climb into second behind the Cardinals. Dwight was once again selected for the All-Star Game, but couldn't pitch because he had pitched the day before.

But even with the tight races taking place in all the divisions of both leagues, the focus of attention was not on the pennant races! The bigger problem was if there would even be a season after August 6. That was the day the players, who had been threatening to strike, walked out. Dwight, who had managed to win his seventeenth game on a five-hitter against the Cubs and to set a club record with his eleventh straight win, could only feel good that the Mets were in first. So, no matter what happened, the team was in a good position if the league decided to have a split season as it did in the strike year of 1981. This time, however, there would be no split season. Commissioner Peter Ueberroth stepped in and helped resolve the strike after 2 days. The season was back on!

After the strike scare, Dwight won his thirteenth straight game to put his record at an amazing 19–3. Then, on Sunday, August 25, Dwight took the mound at Shea against the Expos with a chance to become the youngest twenty-game winner ever in the major leagues. But there was a fine mist falling, and Dwight found it difficult to grip the ball.

In the third inning, leading 3–0 as a result of a first-inning spree by the Mets, Dwight lost control of the ball and threw 2 wild pitches. He also made a throwing error that led to two Montreal runs. Considering that he had only thrown 3 wild pitches all season, it was obvious that the rain was dramatically affecting his performance. And where Dwight could usually coast on a three-run cushion, today he was struggling. After Darryl Strawberry hit his twentieth homer of the season in the fifth, Montreal came back in the sixth to score yet another run off Dwight.

With the score now at 4–3 after 6 full innings, Manager Davey Johnson took Dwight out of the game. In his last start, the Doctor had thrown 149 pitches in chalking up 16 K's against the Giants. In this game, he had already thrown 94 pitches, allowing 5 hits and 1 walk with 4 strikeouts. Davey Johnson was not about to take a chance on hurting his young ace's arm by allowing him to go any further.

As Dwight sat in the dugout, waiting to see if reliever Roger McDowell could hold the lead and save the victory, the Mets went on to score 4 more runs in the bottom of the seventh to break the game wide open. Then the Mets scored another run in the eighth and McDowell held the Expos to 1 in his 3 innings of work. When the game was over, Dwight had his twentieth win!

The large crowd would not let Dwight go to the clubhouse without stepping out of the dugout to receive a well-deserved standing ovation. After all, at 20 years, 9 months and 9 days, Dwight had put his name into the record books as the youngest twenty-game winner ever! In winning his fourteenth straight, he had beaten the major league record by almost a month. In 1938, Hall of Famer Bob Feller, pitching for the Cleveland Indians, had won his twentieth game at the age of 20 years, 10 months and 5 days. And in breaking that record, Dwight also established the majors' longest winning streak of the year.

In the clubhouse, General Manager Frank Cashen gave Dwight a special gift from the Mets. It was a "20" marked out in baseballs on a large board. To the crowd of reporters, wanting to know how he felt about the record, Dwight said, "I'm thankful for my team." Teammate Gary Carter best summed up the feelings of the Mets, the fans and anyone who enjoys baseball when he said, "We're all fortunate to be part of Dwight's little world." What the catcher meant was that it was a thrill to be so close to someone who performs at such a high level and who remains humble about his accomplishments.

Despite the Mets' hard charge, when August came to a close, they were still 2 games behind the Cardinals. And after winning 14 games in a row and compiling a record of 20–3, Dwight lost to the lowly Giants at Candlestick Park by a 3–2 score. It was his first defeat in nearly 2 months!

Dwight immediately began another incredible streak, this time involving not victories—he would be involved in tight-pitched heartbreakers—but innings pitched without allowing an earned run. The streak began on September 6 in a game against Fernando Valenzuela and the Dodgers in Los Angeles. Dwight struck out 10 and gave up only 5 hits. He left the game after the ninth with the score tied 0–0. Valenzuela kept the Mets at bay through the eleventh inning as the Dodgers went on to win 2–0 in the thirteenth. In Dwight's next start against John Tudor and the Cards, Dwight pitched another 9 scoreless innings only to have another no-decision as the Cardinals won in the tenth on a home run by César Cedeño off of Jesse Orosco. Dwight could have been forgiven if he had sued the Mets' batters for lack of support! Two shutouts and no victories to show for his efforts! Dwight ran his scoreless-innings streak to 31 and finally picked up his twenty-first win by blanking the Phillies at Shea on a two-hit gem. Yet, even with Dwight pitching flawlessly and chalking up his twenty-second and twenty-third victories, the Mets still found themselves 3 games out on October 1 when they went into St. Louis to play a crucial three-game series against the first-place Cardinals in the last week of the season. The division title was on the line, and the Mets needed to sweep all 3 games.

Ron Darling pitched brilliantly in the series opener, besting the Cardinals' ace, John Tudor, and moved the Mets to within 2 games of the Cards. It was then Dwight's turn. His mound opponent was Andujar, who had a 21–10 record going into the game. In front of another capacity crowd of almost 50,000 people on hand, the Mets scored first and then added another run in the top of the second when Dwight took first on a fielder's choice that would have been a double play had Dwight not hustled to first base. But in the bottom of the second, Dwight's earned-run scoreless streak ended at 49 innings—the longest in the majors for the year—when the Cardinals' catcher, Darrell Porter, hit a triple to score Andy Van Slyke, who had led off the inning with a single. With Porter on third and only 1 out, Dwight induced Ozzie Smith to line out to Howard Johnson at third, and then he struck out Andujar, stranding Porter at third base.

Dwight stopped another St. Louis threat in the fifth when Porter doubled with 2 outs and he again struck out Andujar. The Mets added another run in their half of the fifth to make the score 3–1, and then pushed the score to 5–1 in the seventh, 1 of the runs coming on George Foster's twenty-first home run of the year. In the bottom of the ninth, base-stealing sensation Vince Coleman gave the Cardinals some hope when he batted in Smith, but Dwight—as he had done all evening—slammed the door on the Cards for a 5–2 win, his twenty-fourth of the season! Not only had Dwight struck out 10, but he was credited with 2 sacrifice hits. More important, the Mets were within 1 game of first place.

Although the victory was not Dwight's best performance of the year (he had given up 9 hits), it was by far the most important game of his short career. There wasn't much more anyone on the team could ask of him, short of being able to come back and pitch the next night. Of course, that was not really possible. And, unfortunately, the Mets lost the last game of the series, allowing St. Louis to increase their lead to 2 full games with only 3 to play. But for Dwight, who had almost single-handedly brought the Mets a divisional championship, there was little he could do but hope for a miracle in the final 3 days of the season.

The Mets returned home to face Montreal while the Cards stayed in St. Louis to take on the Cubs. The Mets won their first game, but so did the Cards. The next day, the Cards won again and it was all over. The Mets lost, but even if they had won, it wouldn't have mattered.

Even though the Mets had lost, everyone, including the fans and manager Davey Johnson, thought it had been a great season. And everyone showed his appreciation for each other the next day—the last day of the 1985 season—when after another meaningless loss, the Mets fans gave the team a standing ovation and the players responded by tipping their caps to the fans. Some players even threw their caps into the stands as souvenirs.

Dwight had had a spectacular year. He led the major leagues with an incredible 1.53 earned-run average, 268 strikeouts, and 24 victories. This incredible achievement, leading the major leagues in ERA, strikeouts and victories—the pitching "triple crown"—is so rare that it has only been accomplished by 7 pitchers (the last one to do it was Sandy Koufax, who did it in 1966 after doing it in 1965 and 1963). Sandy Koufax, the ex-Dodger Hall of Famer, is regarded by many people as the greatest left-handed pitcher of all time. So Dwight is in pretty fancy company, and the amazing thing about all of this is that Koufax didn't win his first "triple" until he was 28 years old, and Dwight won his when he was still 20.

On November 13, 3 days before his 21st birthday, Dwight received an early birthday present—the Cy Young Award! He is the youngest player to ever win pitching's highest honor. He received all of the first place votes cast and thereby became only the seventh pitcher in the history of baseball to win the award by a unanimous vote.

Although Dwight is delighted by the praise and the awards he gets for his pitching, he loves to talk about his hitting. Like many pitchers, hitting is the subject that is really closest to his heart. He even claims to have more power from the left side of the plate than Strawberry, his roommate on the road. Strawberry, of course, does not take his right-handed-hitting roommate seriously. But Dwight was seen rounding the bases with a huge smile on his face when he hit his first career home run on September 21 at Shea Stadium against Rick Rhoden of the Pirates. After that, all Strawberry could say was, "He'll never let us forget it." And Dwight shocked the reporters when he said, "I'd rather hit a home run than throw a no-hitter." Although he might have hit only 1 home run, he did go on to set a season record for Mets' pitchers with a total of 21 base hits.

When you talk about Dwight's pitching abilities, you talk about something really special. As Mets' announcer Tim McCarver, a former big league star who caught Hall of Famer Bob Gibson and played against Sandy Koufax, considered the best southpaw to ever pitch in the majors, says, "For one year, the greatest pitcher I ever saw was Gibson. Over seven years, Sandy Koufax was the greatest I ever saw ... and Gooden has the potential to be better than both of them." Koufax, himself, put it even shorter: "I would trade my past for Gooden's future."

It's hard to imagine how much more this incredibly gifted athlete will accomplish in the years to come because there doesn't appear to be any ceiling on his talent. Maybe he'll go back to playing third base on the days he doesn't pitch and head the league in batting and home runs.

Whatever lies ahead, it will be a thrill to watch the good "doctor" dazzle us for years to come as he rewrites baseball's record books.

Dwight Gooden showing perfect form as a 19-year-old rookie.
UPI/Bettmann Newsphotos

Dwight tips his cap to the fans who were applauding his fine
effort in striking out 14 Dodgers on his way to a 2–1 victory.

AP/Wide World Photos

The youngest and the oldest performers in the 1984 All-Star
game: Dwight Gooden and Phil Niekro of the Yankees.
AP/Wide World Photos

Dwight is smiling because his 16 strikeouts just gave him the all-time major league strikeout record for a rookie—September 12, 1984.
UPI/Bettmann Newsphotos

Posing with Mets' chairman of the board, Nelson Doubleday, after winning Rookie-of-the-Year award.
AP/Wide World Photos

The rewards of success. Signing a hefty contract while his proud father and happy Mets' General Manager, Frank Cashen, look on.
UPI/Bettmann Newsphotos

New Met Gary Carter smiling because he won't have to bat
against Dwight Gooden anymore.
AP/Wide World Photos

Great concentration and a 2–0 shutout for Dwight's 16th victory—July 30, 1985.
AP/Wide World Photos

Pitchers always want to be hitters and Dwight is a good hitter.
Focus on Sports

Beating the Cardinals for his 24th victory—October 2, 1985.
UPI/Bettmann Newsphotos

Going, going, gone! Another home run for Dale Murphy.
AP/Wide World Photos

Dale Murphy and Cal Ripken of the Orioles holding their
1983 M.V.P. plaques.
UPI/Bettmann Newsphotos

Dale launches a home run during 1984 All-Star game...
UPI/Bettmann Newsphotos

And gets a smile and a handshake from Dodgers' manager, Tommy Lasorda.
UPI/Bettmann Newsphotos

Great try, but no catch.
AP/Wide World Photos

This one didn't get away.
AP/Wide World Photos

Dale and his wife Nancy smiling after Dale had been named
M.V.P. for 1984.
AP/Wide World Photos

The youngest player to ever win back-to-
back M.V.P. awards.
AP/Wide World Photos

DALE MURPHY

1

The Next Johnny Bench

To look at Dale Murphy playing center field today, with his deerlike speed and strong throwing arm, you'd think it was a position he was born to play. But that's not where Dale started when he first got serious about baseball. He liked all the action that took place behind the plate and decided to become a catcher. As things turned out, it was a move that almost cost him his big league career.

Born on March 12, 1956, in Portland, Oregon, Dale Bryan Murphy was the second child of Charles and Betty Murphy. Their first child, Sue, was 3 years older. Except for the family's brief move to Moraga, California, the senior Murphys always made their home in Portland. Although his parents were supportive and his dad played catch with his young son when he had time away from his job at Westinghouse, Dale's real interest in baseball came from his legendary great-great grandfather. As Dale says, "He wasn't only a semipro baseball player who caught, but a bronco rider and a trick roper to boot."

One generation closer to Dale is his grandfather (on his mother's side), Ledger Bryan, who was an Oklahoma farmer during the Great Depression of the 1930's, and also played baseball. Yet as Popo (as he is affectionately called) will admit, "I was better known in the field than at the plate." One thing for certain, he is probably Dale's biggest fan. Although he is 68 years old now, he still jumps on a plane to see Dale play in person whenever the urge hits him.

Other than baseball, Dale played all sports as a boy and even spent 1 season on his high school football team alternating between tight end and tailback. But when you ask Dale about his boyhood and his deep interest in sports, he makes a point of saying, "The most important thing is to have fun, to enjoy every sport you play...and not to take it seriously until you are paid for it." It is a piece of advice that Dale learned from his parents when they first enrolled him in Little League when he was around 10. At that time he instantly made news by getting a hit his first time up against John Dunn, known for throwing 17 no-hitters in the Little League!

It was John Dunn's father, Jack, who first saw the real potential in Dale. Jack Dunn was the high school baseball coach at Woodrow Wilson High in Portland (now coaching in college at Portland State in Oregon). But in those days all Dale could boast of was a strong arm. Still, his basic tools were strong enough to have Jack tell Dale's father, "Have you given any thoughts to your boy being a pro prospect?" Considering that Dale was already 6 feet tall in the seventh grade, with excellent coordination, the idea of his playing pro ball was not that outrageous.

Under Dunn's guidance during high school ball and in the summer American Legion program, the young Dale Murphy began to blossom. By the time he was a senior he had reached 6'4" and was throwing out would-be base-stealers with a bullet arm while hitting over .400 and was named All-City and All-State.

Of course it is Jack Dunn to whom Dale owes the most in his athletic development. (Although it is only a coincidence, and he is no relation to Dale's coach, it was a man by the name of Jack Dunn who discovered the immortal Babe Ruth!) When you ask him about Jack, whom he is still close to, Dale will be the first to acknowledge Jack—but not without mentioning his father at the same time: "I owe a lot to my dad. He helped me in all situations and gave me a purpose. Because of him and my mom I learned to keep things in perspective...and that's really important."

By the time the June, 1974, baseball draft rolled around, Dale was certain that he would be picked by the Philadelphia Phillies. Of all the teams that scouted him, they seemed the most interested. But what Dale didn't know was that the Phils were convinced that the catcher from Portland would never hit with power. So when it came to the Phils' turn (they were ahead of Atlanta) their choice was Lonnie Smith (now with the Kansas City Royals). On the Braves' first round they were the fifth team to select in 1974, and Dale was chosen to be the team's catcher of the future. Not bad for an 18-year-old kid who hadn't taken the game seriously until 4 years before!

The Braves gave Dale a signing bonus of $52,000, and rather than go on to Arizona University—the baseball machine that has turned out many a great ballplayer, including Reggie Jackson—Dale decided to get his training in the front lines of the minors. So, after graduation, he packed his bags and headed to Kingsport in the rookie league to finish the season.

All the press notices called him "the next Johnny Bench," and no one could foresee that there would be a drastic change in the script, least of all Dale Murphy!

2

To the Minors and Back Again

One of the things that Dale Murphy didn't know when he joined the Atlanta organization was that the Braves' scouting reports were pretty much in agreement with what the Phils' scouts had said: "It is doubtful that he'll develop into a power hitter." Only one of the Braves' scouts saw any potential in Dale's bat. But as Paul Snyder, the Braves' director of scouting, recalls of those early reports, "We took him because of his defensive abilities and athletic skills." So much for experts!

It seemed as though the reports on Dale might be right. In his first year in 54 games and 181 at bats, he only hit 5 home runs. But in the spring of 1975 when Dale was called on to catch an exhibition game against Atlanta, he nailed every Braves runner who attempted to steal! It was that year (1975) when Dale was promoted to Greenwood, Class A, in the Western Carolina League, but his batting average dropped from .254 the previous year to a disappointing .228 with only 5 homers in 443 at bats. For Dale, who was accustomed to a better performance, it was not a good time.

But an event after the season proved more important to Dale than the season itself, or any season for that matter. It was then, in 1975, that teammate Barry Bonnell, now with the Seattle Mariners, baptized Dale into the Church of Latter-day Saints. Becoming a Mormon was an important move for him. As he says, "I think every person wants to lead a good life. Inside every person there is a conscience telling him to follow it to good things. I felt in my heart that I wanted to be part of the Church." Considering the bumpy road that still lay ahead for him, it was a decision that helped him in his struggle to reach the majors and in his personal life as well.

When 1976 rolled around, the Braves had enough faith to place him on the Savannah roster, a Class AA team in the Southern League. It seemed that, even with his problems at the plate, the Braves knew it would only be a matter of time. With his average at .267 and 12 home runs, he was promoted during the same season to Triple A ball, where he played for Richmond in the International League, only one stop from the big team. There, he hit .260 and had 4 home runs in 18 games. He even hit an extra-inning pinch grand slam that helped the Richmond Braves earn a playoff spot. It was enough of a showing for Atlanta to give him a taste of the majors after the minor league playoffs were over.

In his first game, at Dodger Stadium, there were 40,000 people in the stands, more people than Dale had ever played in front of. Was he nervous? When he now recalls the game, he laughs at just how nervous he was. Even the hit he got off Rick Rhoden, now with the Pittsburgh Pirates, was nothing to write home about. As Dale puts it, "I got an infield single on a swinging bunt." Or at least it seemed like that, since Dale had had no intention of bunting.

The Braves were impressed enough with Dale's raw talent that they projected him to be their regular catcher for the 1977 season. But when next season began, Dale found himself back with Richmond in the International League!

His problem: he suddenly couldn't throw out base-stealers. His throws were scattered all over the field. While some hit in front of the pitching mound, others went on one hop to the outfielders. Only his dad could lighten the situation a little by saying, "If second base were in center field, Dale would throw everyone out."

Dale's problem was a real mystery to the Braves' management. The Braves had not given up on him, but knew from Dale's showing during that spring training that he needed to work on his throws to second without the pressures of trying to work it out in the big leagues. What few knew at the time was that Dale had almost given up the Braves and baseball to become a missionary in the Church! It was a decision that Dale had wrestled with from the end of the 1976 season up until 2 months before the start of spring training of the 1977 season. As a result, he was a hold-out! Only the urging of the Mormon Church and the pleas of Braves' owner Ted Turner kept him in the game. As Dale says, "Religion is really important to me, but I decided it was best to stay in baseball. By doing so, I would be able to reach a lot of young people."

Today when you ask Dale about 1977, he will tell you it was his most frustrating year. But he never gave up working toward his goal, and back in Richmond he led the league with 33 doubles and 90 RBIs! Once again, the Braves brought him up after the September roster expansion. And this time in 18 games he had 2 home runs while hitting for a .316 average. Even though he still had problems behind the plate, the Braves were ready to give Dale a full-time shot with the club, either with the catcher's mitt or the first baseman's glove (where he had played some in the minors). The Braves were in need of some new talent—having spent the last 7 years out of the pennant race—and their first home-grown product seemed ready for the start of the 1978 season. Or at least they hoped so!

3

The Newest Brave

Dale's first full season (1978) in the uniform of the Atlanta Braves was not without its problems. His throwing arm was still erratic, and the experiment of placing him at first base was even more of a failure. Of the 151 games he played for the Braves, 129 games found him at first. Unfortunately, he led the league in errors.

As one writer later wrote about Dale, "Without a mask, the folks in the stands could see whom they were booing." Even Dale's father was led to observe, "I thought he was done." The Braves had just about given up on Dale as a catcher, and his size 13 shoes did nothing to help his agility at first. But where Dale's defensive abilities were disappointing, his offensive contribution did not go without notice. The 22-year-old managed to bat in 79 runs and send 23 home runs over the fence while hitting a somewhat disappointing .226. It was enough of a showing to cause Hank Aaron, the team's vice-president and the greatest home-run hitter of all time, to comment: "I think he's the most gifted athlete on the team, bar none. The fact that he had a low batting average was a blessing in disguise. If he can drive in seventy-nine runs and hit twenty-three homers hitting in the low two hundreds, think what he'll do after he's worked on his average some." And Rex Bowen, the Cincinnati Reds' superscout, said after watching Dale in spring training, "That's the kind of kid you build a franchise around."

His RBIs led the team, and his home runs tied team-mates Bob Horner and Jeff Burroughs for the club high. But another problem was that Dale—in reaching for the seats—also led the league in strikeouts with a whopping 145 whiffs.

Rather than worry in the off-season about what 1979 would have in store, Dale found a more positive direction. Since he had passed up a scholarship to play pro ball, he thought it was a good time to brush up on his education and enroll at Brigham Young University. It was there, while studying public relations, that he met Nancy Thomas, his future wife. In what has become known as "typical Dale Murphy modesty," Nancy wasn't even aware that he played for the Braves. As she says, "I thought he was a semipro ballplayer." The next October, 1979, Dale and Nancy married in Temple Square in Salt Lake City.

As far as the season of 1979 was concerned, his marriage to Nancy after the season was the only high point worth remembering. The Braves had another terrible year and again finished last in the National League West. Dale played in only 104 games because he tore cartilage in his knee while trying to chase a knuckleball. The injury really hurt because, only a week before, on May 18, Dale had had the greatest home-run game of his short career when he hit 3 out against the San Francisco Giants. It was only the sixth time the feat had been accomplished by an Atlanta player!

By season's end Dale was able to hit only 21 homers, but it was only 2 less than the year before when he had had almost 150 more at bats. The Braves now knew they had a potential superstar and great home-run hitter. Paul Snyder, the head of the Braves' scouts, noted, "I don't think we have any idea how good the real Murphy can be. The real Murphy is not here yet.

In 1980 he'll arrive. I just hope the good Lord lets me live long enough to see that, because he'll be a sight to behold."

Snyder was almost right about Dale becoming a superstar the next year, especially because of a move made by Bobby Cox, then manager of the Braves. The solution was to place Murphy—who couldn't master catching or first base—into left field. As Cox said, "Because we tried all our other ideas, I decided to see what would happen if we put him in left field." It so happened that the move came in an exhibition game on March 12, Dale's 24th birthday! He instantly responded by nailing a runner trying to score with a perfect strike to the plate. As Dale now says, "It was an immediate confidence boost."

Having mastered left field by midseason, Dale moved to center, where his great speed and arm could make even more of a contribution to the team. Dale's performance earned him a spot on the National League All-Star team, and the Braves moved up 2 notches to fourth in their division. Dale's home-run total passed the 30 barrier for the first time as he finished third in the league with 33 to Bob Horner who hit 35 and Mike Schmidt of the Phillies who hit 48. Dale was also honored by being named National League Player of the Month for August. Finally, it seemed that Dale Murphy, the ex-Johnny Bench hopeful, was on his way to fulfilling his own destiny.

Dale and Nancy, then living in a suburb of Atlanta, had their first child that fall. It was a boy. They named him Chad, and then Travis was born in 1981, and Shawn in 1982. They may follow in their dad's footsteps. But chances are they may have some competition, because Dale believes that "a ten-child family is possible."

When the 1981 season got under way, most of the

baseball talk was focused on a threatened strike. Finally, when the owners and the players could not reach agreement, the players walked out and one-third of the season was lost. For Dale, who only managed to hit .247 with 13 RBIs, it might have been better if the season never took place at all. His one highlight was tying for the league lead among outfielders by throwing out runners to complete 4 double plays. In the split season that took place because of the strike, the Braves finished fourth in the first half and fifth in the second out of 6 teams in the N.L. West.

It was obvious that if Atlanta were to rise from mediocrity, Dale would have to find a way to return to form.

4
Dale Murphy, MVP

When Dale arrived in spring training for the start of the 1982 season, Bobby Cox, the Braves' manager since 1978, was no longer holding the reins. Instead, Joe Torre, who had starred for the Cardinals and Mets, and had also managed the Mets, was now the new manager. And for the Braves, who had not finished in the top half of their division since 1974—and not won a division title since 1969—it turned out to be a banner year. And the man responsible for leading the Braves out of the darkness and into the light was the one and only Dale Murphy!

The Braves started the season in a blaze by winning their first 13 games, a new major league record for consecutive wins at the start of a season. That opening drive turned out to be an omen as the Braves finally captured their divisional title.

In helping the Braves take the National League West flag, Dale played every game on Atlanta's one hundred sixty-two-game schedule (something no Brave had managed to do since Felix Millan in 1969). But that was just for openers! Dale tied Montreal's Al Oliver for the league lead in RBIs (109), ranked second in homers (36) and runs scored (113), fourth in walks (93), seventh in slugging percentage (.507), tied for ninth in game-winning RBIs (14) and finished tenth in on-base percentage (.378). He even won the league's Gold Glove Award (for the best defensive player at his position). Dale was also voted by the fans to start for the National League All-Star team. And to put the icing on the cake, he was selected as the National League's Most Valuable Player.

Dale Murphy had finally arrived! And he did it despite the fact that, during one stretch in August, he hit only .177 for 21 games. But when he wasn't contributing at the plate, he was more than making up for it in the field, saving many games with diving catches, leaping catches and strong throws. It was the kind of play that caused manager Joe Torre to say, "Power hitters are often a hindrance when they're going bad, but in Murphy's case, the opposite is true." The only disappointment came in the championship playoffs, where the Braves lost to the Cardinals.

In winning the MVP award, Dale placed first on 14 of 24 ballots and beat out runner-up Lonnie Smith by a 283–218 margin. It was an ironic turnaround, considering that Smith, then with the Cardinals, was originally selected over Murphy in the 1974 draft by the Phillies! Dale also happened to be the fourth Brave and youngest National League player to win MVP honors for two consecutive years.

So what does Dale do before the start of the next season? Simple, he goes to the instructional league with the rookies to start working on his hitting! What actually happened was that Torre made the suggestion, but as Dale says, "I thought it was a compliment that Joe wanted to take the time and go down there and work on a few things with me."

What Torre wanted Dale to do was become more selective at the plate. "You wouldn't even ask too many MVPs to go to the instructional league, because you know they would resent the idea. But Murphy is different. Special. One of a kind," said Torre before adding: "As good as he was last year, I could see that he could do better. I can see Dale's ability a lot better than he can. He has no idea how good he is—or how good he's going to be. There's no reason that Dale won't be one of the all-time greats in this game."

Another thing that changed in Dale's favor was his salary. When he had his off season in 1981, the Braves wanted to cut his pay by the legal 20 percent, but didn't at the urging of his agent, Bruce Terch. Of course, with the set of statistics Dale had in 1982, he not only kept his salary of $320,000 but got another $40,000 in bonuses! It also turned out to be the year of Dale's free agency, which meant that he could sign with any team, and the Braves quickly agreed to a whopping 8 million dollars over 5 years. Dale suddenly found himself in the special circle of megabuck players. It was a lot of money for the middle-class kid from Portland, but money can't cause him to change his attitude about baseball: "It's like getting paid to go out and play at recess. All my life, I've loved to play baseball, even when I was a kid. This is the same thing, only on a bigger scale."

Dale also happily turned over 10 percent of his salary to the Church. It is something that Dale has done since his conversion in 1975.

The contract made him the fifth-highest-paid player in baseball history, a fact that he is almost apologetic about: "Salaries, I'm the first to admit, are kind of crazy. I mean, it's not like we are firemen or doctors, people who really do important things."

What Dale had learned in the instructional league he quickly put to use for the opening of the 1983 season when, against Tom Niedenfuer of the Dodgers, he won the game in the ninth on a sacrifice fly. For Torre, it proved his point. "Last year, Dale would have struck out in that situation. That's the big difference this year—He is becoming a much better hitter with two strikes on him."

As far as the rest of the league was concerned, Dale

had improved beyond his MVP year. Aside from winning his second consecutive Gold Glove Award, he led the league in RBIs with 121, had another 36 home runs, and once again played in all 162 Braves games. And for the first time, his average for a full season was above .300 (.302). To add to his glowing figures, he also stole 30 bases. It was only the fourth time in National League history and only the sixth time in major league history that anybody had hit 30 or more homers and stolen 30 or more bases in the same season. It was also the first time that anyone—including the great Hank Aaron—had done it for the Braves. Oh yes, he was also the *only* unanimous choice on the first annual UPI All-Star team and missed by only one vote from being a unanimous selection on the AP All-Star team.

Dale's incredible performance earned him his second consecutive MVP award. This time he was named on 21 of the 24 first-place ballots and won easily over Montreal's Andre Dawson, by a 318–213 margin. Dawson, of course, was gracious enough to say, "If you can't be impressed by Murph, you can't be impressed. What really impresses me is how he started out as a catcher a few years back and ends up in center field with a Gold Glove. You've got to appreciate that kind of talent." And Dale's reply: "It was a nice compliment, but I don't belong in Andre's class."

The Braves, however, with another injury to Bob Horner, their slugging third baseman, could do no better than finish the year in second place, 3 games behind the Dodgers. While the 27-year-old Murphy was excited and happy to win the MVP honors and become only the ninth man in baseball history to win the award in back-to-back years, he still doesn't consider it to be his biggest honor. As Dale says, "The MVP Award was nice. But of all the awards, the one

51

that meant the most to me, the one that's really special, is the Exemplary Manhood Award I received in Utah last winter." Dale loves playing baseball, but he loves trying to be the best person that he can be even more.

Before the ink in the record books was dry, Dale received a string of praise from those who knew him, those who played with him and, more important, those who played against him. Hank Aaron dubbed him "the best player in baseball"; Cubs pitching coach Billy Connor added that he was "the best player I've seen since Willie Mays." That's very high praise when you realize that Mays is considered to be one of the best all-around players in the history of the game. Russ Nixon, then the Cincinnati manager, commented, "He's scary. Do they have something above MVP?" George Bamberger, who managed the Mets in 1983, best summed it up by saying, "Last year he was our league's most valuable player. And this year he may be the most improved player in the league. What does that make him?"

For one thing, it didn't make Dale feel above any of his teammates. "I don't feel special. I'm just one of the twenty-five guys on the Atlanta Braves." The proof of Dale's humility may well be in the fact that he didn't even find the need to put his MVP plaques on the wall...or any place else in sight. The 2 plaques that do hang on the wall in the Murphy household are somewhat different: "Families are Forever" and "A man never stands taller than when he is on his knees."

Former teammate Jerry Royster (now with San Diego), in speaking for the players, gave a more accurate description of the MVP—at least as it applies to Dale: "The guys respect him. He's more than Most Valuable Player—he's the Most Valuable Person."

5

A Sight to Behold!

Dale Murphy was no longer the kid with the promise.

Dale Murphy was now the superstar with the Braves. He not only fulfilled his early promise, but went far beyond that to become not only respected at the plate and in the field, but also off the field as a very special "one of a kind." Or, in the words of Paul Snyder, "a sight to behold!"

There was, however, one problem. After winning the MVP honors the last 2 seasons, they expected him to do it again! To say the least, it was incredible pressure. After all, no one in baseball history had been able to perform that feat. Already, Dale's statistics over the past 2 seasons were impressive enough for a possible future trip to Cooperstown and the Baseball Hall of Fame; 72 home runs, 230 RBIs, 244 runs scored and a .292 batting average. And all those great numbers don't include the games he won with his great defensive ability. Winning a third straight MVP would almost cinch it.

Yet, as Dale and the Braves got off to their 1984 campaign, Murphy's batting average fell to a low of .130 for the month of April. He had failed to realize what the success of the past 2 seasons would mean. He and his wife, Nancy, and their 3 children had been overrun by admiring fans. Not just after the ballgame, but at his home as well! Since Dale is the kind of guy who can't say no, either to a reporter's question or a fan wanting an autograph, the Murphys found themselves with no time for themselves. It even got so bad that on one occasion when the family came home, they found some fans wandering through the house waiting for Dale's return. Besides losing all privacy, Nancy had suffered 2 recent miscarriages. Also, Travis, their second child, born in 1981 with a rare disease that retards mental and physical development, had caught pneumonia and had to undergo surgery in 1983.

To add to the pressure on the field, Dale's teammate Bob Horner was injured with a broken wrist, and of course was unable to play. Without Horner's big bat behind him, Dale wouldn't get to see as many good pitches to hit. Pitchers could pitch around him, or nibble at the corners and try to make him hit their pitch. The pressure in the locker room consisted of the big IF—Was he going to make MVP for a third time? As he recalls, "Maybe I began to think that it was important for me to make that goal. That was the wrong thing to do....I was playing for all the wrong reasons." But Dale—who has never been thrown out of a game and will confess to only once arguing with a minor league umpire—reached the height of his frustrations on August 9 when, in a home game against the Dodgers, he struck out for the hundredth time. Returning to the dugout, he "drop-kicked" the plastic water cooler, and ice went everywhere. The act, totally out of character, shocked his teammates. It also shocked Dale. Later that night, when he told Nancy about the incident, he realized that something was terribly wrong. "It woke me up to what I was doing to myself," he said. "I was much too intense. That kind of intensity, too much up or down, ends up getting to you."

So for a guy who couldn't say no (even to a fan that got hit by a Murphy foul ball and who then asked Dale to autograph his bruise), Dale decided to relax at the plate and at home. The result was almost immediate. Dale's bat was red-hot enough in September that he was voted the National League Player of the Month! Considering what his final stats were, it is amazing to think what kind of year he would have had or what his chances might have been for a third straight MVP award if he hadn't allowed the pressure to get to him earlier in the season. Dale led the league in games (162), total bases (332) and slugging percentage (.547). In home runs, he tied for first with Mike Schmidt by hitting 36 for the third time in 3 years. He was also third in the league with 100 RBIs. Dale also happened to win his third straight Gold Glove Award. The last National League player to win a gold glove and a home-run title in the same year just happened to be Dale's first idol, Willie Mays!

As an extra added footnote, Dale went 2 for 3 in the All-Star Game and hit his first homer of the midsummer classic off of Detroit's Willie Hernandez, who just happened to win the American League's Cy Young Award and MVP that year. Also, by playing in all the Braves' games, Dale finished the year with 495 consecutive games, which was the longest such streak at that time. In addition to getting the thousandth base hit of his short career, Dale also pulled off a rare feat. On May 27, he hit home runs off the Cardinals' Joaquin Andujar (a twenty-game winner for the year) and Bruce Sutter, the league's premier relief pitcher. Sutter said admiringly, "The guy is just awesome." The Dodgers' Orel Hershiser, who had a thirty-four-inning scoreless streak broken up by Dale on August 30 with a home run, just shook his head dejectedly.

Dale's homers, by the way, did not all come in the snug confines of Atlanta–Fulton County Stadium. He hit 18 of his 36 round-trippers on the road, 6 of which came in the tough Houston Astrodome, a record for visiting players. After all the disappointment of the early going, it seemed like an MVP performance, especially to Joe Torre: "You can put him in a class with a [Willie] Mays and a [Hank] Aaron because he can beat you with his glove, and he can beat you with a home run."

But the sportswriters who do the voting had a different notion, and Ryne Sandberg, who led the Cubs to a divisional title, won the MVP award in 1984. "Big Number 3" just couldn't carry the Braves past a tie with Houston for second, 12 games behind the Padres—and the poor showing by Atlanta didn't help Dale's chances.

One of the things that the Murphys had to do at the end of the season was try and find some privacy where they could just function as a family. They wound up moving to a secluded spot in the country, 40 miles from the stadium. There, nestled in the trees, Dale could play ball with his 3 sons and tend the garden. To know how good a move it was, you only have to hear Nancy's comment before the start of the 1985 season: "We just had the greatest off-season. He's looser now."

Good for the Murphys, bad for the National League!

6

Headin' for Cooperstown

Two major changes in the Braves' structure gave the fans some hope that the team would challenge the Padres and the other Western Division teams for first place in 1985. The team had made a heavy investment by picking up premier relief pitcher Bruce Sutter in the free-agency pool (at a salary of 2 million a year). They also installed Eddie Haas as manager.

Haas had been successful as a manager in the Braves' farm system and was thought to have the tools to send the Braves over the top. Haas was able to make a quick contribution by having Dale alter his hitting style slightly, and the effects were immediate and sensational. Dale simply tore up the league's pitching staff.

In the month of April, the All-Star center fielder hit 11 home runs and drove in 29 RBIs, plus he led the league in 5 other offensive categories! To add some icing on the cake, the 29 runs he batted in tied Ron Cey's major league record for the month of April. Cey, now with the Cubs, did it in 20 games, while Dale did it in just 19. It was such an impressive performance that Pete Rose said, "These days, anytime one of my pitchers keeps Murphy in the ballpark, I pat 'im on the fanny." Baseball's all-time hit leader also was moved to tell Dale himself, "You're the best player in the league. That's all there is to it."

And that's not just Pete Rose's opinion. For the last 5 years, the Elias Sports Bureau has ranked each player at his position; and in a not very large surprise, the combined statistics for the 1984 and 1985 seasons show that Dale was number one in the outfield group.

Luke Appling, the Braves' hitting instructor and Hall of Famer, predicted that Dale would hit 70 home runs in 1985. Of course, Dale was the first to deny such a possibility. Not that he isn't capable of such a feat, but because hitting home runs is only a small part of what he's all about.

At 29, the 6'5", 215-pound Atlanta star qualifies as one of today's baseball superstars. But for the man who is referred to as the "Gentle Giant" and "John-Boy" (after the character in *The Waltons*), the outstanding thing is the 1,000 batting average he hits off the field! As his former teammate and three hundred-game winner Phil Niekro (late of the New York Yankees) says, "People keep looking for words to describe him. Well, there aren't enough good words or words good enough."

Dale's terrific start helped him to another incredible year, which included leading the league outright in home runs for the first time with 37 while driving in 111 runs (second in the league), marking his fourth consecutive year of 100 or more RBIs. In slugging percentage, he was third with a .539 mark, and in the all-important on-base percentage category—which includes hits, walks and times hit by a pitch—Dale was fifth with an impressive .388 average. His 185 hits—a career high—placed him fifth in the league. Of course, he easily led the Braves in almost every offensive category, and he was also the leading vote-getter for the All-Star Game. Dale also happened to play in all of the Braves' games once again to extend his consecutive playing streak to 657 games.

With the kind of physical condition that Dale keeps himself in—the key to any athlete's staying power—the thought around baseball is that the 29-year-old superstar may well extend his "prime years" beyond the norm and have the chance to rack up even more impressive stats. As Hank Aaron says, "It's because he's kept himself in such great condition. He's like a Cadillac. He's streamlined. He knows what he can and can't do and what it takes.... The body of a twenty-year-old."

As for Dale, he says, "The biggest thing to me is the attitude now. Last year was good ... because I learned the value of having a good one hundred sixty-two-game attitude. It takes a few years to acquire that. You have to go through the ups and downs to learn that."

A big down, despite another fabulous year for Dale individually, was the failure of the Braves to seriously challenge the Dodgers for the divisional title; they wound up in fifth place. Bruce Sutter, who was supposed to be the stopper in the bull pen, had an off year and an injured arm. And even Eddie Haas didn't survive the disaster, as he was replaced after the season by former Pirates' manager Chuck Tanner.

While most ballplayers would gladly trade for Murphy's career—even as it stands right now—he thinks that it's too early to make any judgment: "I've had a couple of good years. My goal is to have a good career, and I haven't gotten there yet."

Maybe not, but with the achievements that Dale has already accomplished and the bright future ahead of him, Dale seems destined to achieve the game's highest honor—a place in the Hall of Fame!

But for the man whose only endorsements include milk commercials for a local Atlanta company (Kinnett Dairy), a baseball glove for Rawlings (the Dale Murphy model) and promotional work for Nike shoes, Cooperstown will only be part of the story of Dale Murphy. The greater part may be off the field, where he freely gives of himself on every possible occasion.

Dale is a deeply religious man. He sets his priorities by naming his family first and baseball second. He doesn't drink, curse, smoke or chew tobacco. Dale even credits the home runs he hits to luck, his manager, his teammates, and to God. Although it is hard to believe, he even apologized one day when he hit a home run off Bruce Sutter, then with the Cardinals. Dale's comment: "What can I do? If it goes over the fence, I guess it's a home run."

When he is not playing baseball, he gives his time to his family, to charitable organizations such as Cystic Fibrosis and Huntington's Disease, and the Church. He is, of all people, the least impressed by his own accomplishments. Says Dale, "I don't want ever to have people think I'm better than anyone else."

To know that he is one of the team's most popular players, just ask second baseman Glen Hubbard: "The guys love Murph. They respect him for what he believes, and he respects them." One reporter, when trying to see if Dale was really as good as his reputation, could find only that he once was stopped for speeding. He was driving 35 miles an hour in a 25-mile-per-hour zone. The reason: He was late for a speech he was giving at a church!

Dale may not have any vices, but he does have a weakness when it comes to food. Eating up to 6 times a day—meals, snacks, you name it—he is famous for devouring everything in sight. There really isn't any dish he can say no to, and hardly anything he won't eat in a restaurant except the menu. And even that isn't beyond him, according to his teammates. Oddly enough, Dale—who bats and throws right-handed—uses his left hand when it comes to writing and eating. "I don't know how it happened. It just worked out that way," says Dale.

For Dale Murphy, who has so many friends in so many cities that he's won the Ticketron award four years in a row (given to the Braves' player who uses up the most passes), there is no limit to his concern or generosity. In an incident that took place before a game in June of 1983, Dale visited 6-year-old Elizabeth Smith in the hospital and gave her a cap and a T-shirt. The girl had lost both arms and a leg in a power-line accident during the winter. When the girl's nurse innocently asked if Dale would hit a home run for Elizabeth, he and the girl looked at each other. Dale was caught by such surprise that he could only mumble, "Well, okay." He then hit not one but two home runs and drove in all 3 runs in a 3–2 Braves victory. The one thing that Dale wanted everyone to know was that, as much as he may have wanted to hit those home runs, it was really only a great coincidence. "I wish I could hit home runs on request. I wish I could. But I can't."

But if you really want to know what Dale Murphy is all about, just consider former Braves manager Joe Torre's comment: "If you're a coach, you want him as a player. If you're a father, you want him as a son. If you're a woman, you want him as a husband. If you're a kid, you want him as a father. What else can you say about the guy?"

DWIGHT EUGENE GOODEN
Born November 16, 1964, at Tampa, Fla.
Height, 6.02. Weight, 190
Throws and bats right-handed

Year	Club	League	G.	IP.	W.	L.	Pct.	H.	ER.	SO.	BB.	ERA.
1982—Kingsport	. . . .	Ap'lachian	9	65⅔	5	4	.556	53	18	66	25	2.47
1982—Little Falls	. . .	NYP	2	13	0	1	.000	11	6	18	3	4.15
1983—Lynchburg	. . .	Carolina	27	191	19	4	.826	121	53	300	112	2.50
1984—New York	. . .	National	31	218	17	9	.654	161	63	276	73	2.60
1985—New York	. . .	National	35	276⅔	24	4	.857	198	47	268	69	1.53
Major League Totals			66	494⅔	41	13	.759	359	110	544	142	2.00

ALL-STAR GAME RECORD

Year	League	IP.	W.	L.	Pct.	H.	ER.	SO.	BB.	ERA.
1984—National		2	0	0	.000	1	0	3	0	0.00

DALE BRYAN MURPHY
Born March 12, 1956, at Portland, Ore.
Height, 6.05. Weight, 215
Throws and bats right-handed

Year	Club	League	Pos.	G.	AB.	R.	H.	2B.	3B.	HR.	RBI.	B.A.
1974—Kingsport		Appal.	C	54	181	28	46	7	0	5	31	.254
1975—Greenwood		W. Car.	C-1B	131	443	48	101	20	1	5	48	.228
1976—Savannah		South	C	104	352	37	94	13	5	12	55	.267
1976—Richmond		Int.	C-OF	18	50	10	13	1	1	4	8	.260
1976—Atlanta		Nat.	C	19	65	3	17	6	0	0	9	.262
1977—Richmond		Int.	C-1B	127	466	71	142	33	4	22	90	.305
1977—Atlanta		Nat.	C	18	76	5	24	8	1	2	14	.316
1978—Atlanta		Nat.	1B-C	151	530	66	120	14	3	23	79	.226
1979—Atlanta		Nat.	1B-C	104	384	53	106	7	2	21	57	.276
1980—Atlanta		Nat.	OF-1B	156	569	98	160	27	2	33	89	.281
1981—Atlanta		Nat.	OF-1B	104	369	43	91	12	1	13	50	.247
1982—Atlanta		Nat.	OF	162	598	113	168	23	2	36	109	.281
1983—Atlanta		Nat.	OF	162	589	131	178	24	4	36	121	.302
1984—Atlanta		Nat.	OF	162	607	94	176	32	8	36	100	.290
1985—Atlanta		Nat.	OF	162	616	118	185	32	2	37	111	.300
Major League Totals				1200	4403	724	1225	185	25	237	739	.278

CHAMPIONSHIP SERIES RECORD

Year	Club	League	Pos.	G.	AB.	R.	H.	2B.	3B.	HR.	RBI.	B.A.
1982—Atlanta		Nat.	OF	3	11	1	3	0	0	0	0	.273

ALL-STAR GAME RECORD

Year	League	Pos.	AB.	R.	H.	2B.	3B.	HR.	RBI.	B.A.
1980—National		OF	1	0	0	0	0	0	0	.000
1982—National		OF	2	1	0	0	0	0	0	.000
1983—National		OF	3	0	1	0	0	0	1	.333
1984—National		OF	3	1	2	0	0	1	1	.667
All-Star Game Totals			9	2	3	0	0	1	2	.333

≡AVON ≡SUPERSTARS
where you meet the superstars of your world!

FEATURING 16 pages of dynamite photos

DOUG FLUTIE
75040-6/$2.50 US/$2.95 Can

A close-up look at one of the most celebrated quarterbacks ever to play the game.

DAN MARINO★JOE MONTANA
75039-2/$2.50 US/$2.95 Can

Action-packed biographies of the two best quarterbacks in the N.F.L.—who faced each other in Superbowl XIX.

MAGIC JOHNSON★LARRY BIRD
75095-3/$2.50 US/$2.95 Can

Zoom in on two of basketball's legendary players—the Lakers' "Magic Man" who can't be beat and the Celtics' Bird who may be the finest all-around player ever!

Buy these books at your local bookstore or use this coupon for ordering:

AVON BOOK MAILING SERVICE, P.O. Box 690, Rockville Centre, NY 11571
Please send me the book(s) I have checked above. I am enclosing $ _____
(please add $1.00 to cover postage and handling for each book ordered to a maximum of three dollars). *Send check or money order*—no cash or C.O.D.'s please. Prices and numbers are subject to change without notice. Please allow six to eight weeks for delivery.

Name _____

Address _____

City _____ State/Zip _____

Super 1/86